Other Works by Tim Barker

Anticipating the Return of Christ

At Your Feet

End Times

God's Revelation and Your Future

Mighty Men of Courage from the Bible

My Jesus Journey

My Jesus Journey: Crescendo

My Jesus Journey: Glissando

My Jesus Journey: Rhapsody

Names of God

Our Privilege of Joy

*The Authentic Christian: Revealing Christ through the
Fruit of the Spirit*

The Call of Ephesians

The Lord with Us

The Twelve: Taking Up the Mantle of Christ

The Vision of Nehemiah: God's Plan for Righteous Living

Truth, Love & Redemption: The Holy Spirit for Today

Unified Church

Your Invitation to Christ

Open
Doors

Open
Doors

Tim R. Barker, D. Min.
Network Pastor/Superintendent
South Texas Ministry Network

OPEN DOORS, Barker, Tim.

1st ed.

ISBN: 978-1-7358529-9-7

Dedication

This book is dedicated to my dear friends, Terry & Irma Phipps. Terry, a former Vice President, Nelson University (formerly SAGU) and currently a professor continues to inspire generations. Irma, a key employee of the University for over 30 years partnered in prayer and support with countless students during her service. These two have truly blessed thousands in their ministry pursuits, including me.

For decades, the Phipps have been a source of strength and encouragement to me. Together we've walked through some doors, walked out of some and even closed a few.

Tim R. Barker

Contents

Introduction

Inside or outside.

That's what a door conveys. We stand on one side or the other. We are inside or we are outside.

Here's what else a door conveys, choice. We can open the door or close it. We can keep things inside or force them to remain outside.

Here's one more aspect of a door. It narrows the options for entering or exiting a building. It also means we have a smaller area to guard to ensure that only those we invite enter our business or home.

Not all doors are in walls, however.

The door of opportunity. We all know of that one. It opens to financial success ... or perhaps the marriage altar. It also opens to ministry prospects to bring salvation to the lost.

The door to worship opens by preparation.

Preparation comes through obedience. Obedience transforms us into the image of Christ.

What about emotional doors? We can be locked in or locked out. The doors become prison bars, trapping us in painful situations. How do we find a connection to God when we can't even look up?

Death, the final door in this life. Do you dread it or look forward to what's on the other side?

The door of faithfulness returns us to choice. We may face challenges now, but we can CHOOSE to open the door of faithfulness and SERVE THE LORD.

What doors do you struggle with? This is your opportunity to discover how the doors in your life align with the Word of God. The choice is yours. Decide for Jesus today.

— I —

Home

Doors are extremely important ... without them we could not get into a place or get out! Doors become the way in ... and the way out!

When we understand that everything that comes into our home does so through a door, we can appreciate the symbolic dimension of this event in Exodus and in Deuteronomy about covering the "doorposts" with blood and with God's Word!

Coming In AND Going Out

The symbolism here is powerful ... the entrance to our home where our family lives is to be covered by the "blood of the Lamb." Everything that comes in should pass by the "blood of the Lamb," and everything that leaves out will pass by it also!

Only those homes where the entrance was covered by the blood of the sacrificial lamb were spared the destructive death angel ... and this is still true!

How's the entrance to your home ... how about the door to your heart, too?

We Have a Responsibility

The Bible teaches us that we are responsible to keep the entrance to our heart and home covered with the blood of the Lamb of God ... this alone will keep out the "death" angel!

The Lord said to Moses and Aaron in Egypt, [2] "This month is to be for you the first month, the first month of your year. [3] Tell the whole community of Israel that on the tenth day of this month each man is to take a lamb for his family, one for each household. [4] If any household is too small for a whole lamb, they must share one with their nearest neighbor, having taken into account the number of people there are. You are to determine the amount of lamb needed in accordance with what each person will eat.

— Exodus 12:1-4 —

While all the previous miracles had failed to get Pharaoh to let God's people go, this final one will be the start of a whole new life for Israel!

God's Freedom Miracle

This final contest will be won by applying the "blood of the Lamb" to the doorposts of each home. The only protection for both Egyptian and Jew will be the "blood of the Lamb"... if applied, those inside will be safe! This foreshadows the greater "Lamb of God" to come. Jesus as the "Lamb of God" will shed His blood ... and it too must be applied to the entrance of our heart and our home if we are to be protected by God! This new event will signal freedom from Egypt for Israel ... thus it will become the spiritual new year for them ... from now on they are to mark this "Passover" as the start of their new year! When we get saved, when we apply the "blood of the Lamb" to our own heart and home ... this marks a new beginning for us, too! Their "new year" will begin by leaving slavery and bondage by embarking on a journey to the Promised Land! Ours begins by leaving sin and our old life behind. We are also embarking on a new journey ... one that will take us to heaven.

Salvation Comes by Choice, Not by Birthright

The entire nation of Israel NEEDED to apply the blood if they were to be spared! It did not matter if they were previously circumcised ... the sign of the covenant by circumcision would not spare them from the death angel ... only the "blood of the Lamb!" It did not matter that they were born into God's people ... only the blood would spare them! They all stood in a place of need ... they all needed to apply the blood!

This was one of the rare times when the priests were not responsible for the sacrifices. Each father was responsible for his own home! Each home had to accept their responsibility for following through with this command! For those who had small families, they were instructed to join with others ... salvation was not just for a family, it was shared as the community of God's people ... no one in Israel was to be left out!

The animals you choose must be year-old males without defect, and you may take them from the sheep or the goats. ⁶ Take care of them until the fourteenth day of the month, when all the members of the community of Israel must slaughter them at twilight. ⁷ Then they are to take some of the blood and put it on the sides and tops of the doorframes of the houses where they eat the lambs.

— Exodus 12:5-7 —

The choice of the lamb was very specific ... it had to be a yearling male without any blemish at all! It was to be a perfect specimen ... Jesus was flawless and a perfect specimen of humanity, too! The participation in this was voluntary ... no one would be made to obey, but failure to obey would mean the death of the firstborn son! This was not a decision that could be mulled over for an extended period ... "now is the day of salvation!" There wasn't time to debate the theological questions of why they needed to do this ... it had to be done if they were to save their own sons!

Failure to respond quickly would be costly!

Our Way or God's Way

A failure to comply either by Egyptian or Jew would result in loss ... there was only one thing that would cause the death angel to pass over each house that night, and that one thing was the "blood of the Lamb" applied to the entrance to that home ... and that all were inside the place of safety! Procrastination was not an option ... there was a necessary choice to make ... and time was critical!

It was their choice as to whether they would do things God's way or their own. While this whole thing must have seemed strange to them, obedience would make the difference between life and death ... it still does! The blood was to be applied to the door's side posts and top beam, thus making the shape of a cross! The home's entrance was to be covered by the "blood of the Lamb" ... God help us as Christians to have our home and the entrance to it covered by the

Lamb of God's blood, also!

Today Is Our Time to Choose

God's way or our way. God's way is life. Our way is spiritual death. Only the blood of Christ can keep us aligned with the Word of God.

Have you made the choice to apply the "blood of the Lamb" of God to your home and the entrance to your heart!? This was the father's responsibility here! It is still a call for fathers to be the priests of their home and apply the blood of Christ to all who go in and out of their home!

Have you made the necessary choice, Dad?

That same night they are to eat the meat roasted over the fire, along with bitter herbs, and bread made without yeast. ⁹ Do not eat the meat raw or boiled in water, but roast it over a fire—with the head, legs and internal organs. ¹⁰ Do not leave any of it till morning; if some is left till morning, you must burn it. ¹¹ This is how you are to eat it: with your cloak tucked into your belt, your sandals on your feet and

*your staff in your hand. Eat it in haste; it is the
Lord's Passover.*

— Exodus 12:8-11 —

With the blood's application, they were instructed
to eat bitter herbs to symbolize the bitterness of
slavery that they were about to be delivered from ...
and to eat bread without yeast to symbolize purity and
their haste in leaving! There was no time to debate
issues ... just obey ... no time for yeast! What they were
leaving behind was the bitterness of slavery ... which
had left a bitter taste in their mouths! They were not
to cook the lamb by ordinary means ... this was more
than a dinner ... the lamb was to be considered a sacrifice which was only done by fire! To cook the lamb
in any other way would make it nothing more than
dinner ... it was to be considered as a "sacrifice" to
spare their lives. Therefore, whatever was not eaten
had to be completely burned like a sacrifice! Notice
too that this sacrifice had to be taken in by them ...
while it was available, they had to consume it! This is
true with salvation, too ... while God has provided His
Son as the sacrifice, it is up to us to "consume" Him,

to take Him into our life if salvation is to have merit! He becomes the substitute for our sins ... having a "substitute sacrifice" is a requirement!

A Constant Reminder

The instructions were designed to be a constant reminder to Israel each time they celebrated "Passover" of what God had done for them, so this meal is still served by Jews today to symbolize these truths ... except of course the part about Jesus. It was very important that Israel follow these instructions to the letter! The reason for this was to preserve the meaning of the event without corrupting it ... there could be no wavering from the instructions! This is still true. We cannot reinvent how people should be saved, and it must be by what Christ taught, without compromise!

Communion is the New Testament ordinance that preserves for us the meaning of Jesus' death and life for us ... it is to be kept as Jesus taught so that the meaning is not lost! We are to keep reminders of what Christ has done for us ... this is what communion is all about! The plan must be adhered to without change or compromise if it is to lead to salvation!

Clothes On, Ready to Flee

Notice the instruction on how all this was to be done: They were to eat the sacrifice with their clothes on and ready to leave Egypt! This was no casual meal ... it was meant to be consumed with the idea that they were ready to leave behind their slavery and to leave behind the bondage of Egypt! This is true with Christ, too ... those who receive Christ should do so with the understanding that taking Christ into their life means leaving behind the slavery of sin ... marching out of "Egypt" and going in a new direction ... towards the "Promised Land!"

Deliverance meant just that ... they were delivered from the bondage of slavery. They were not to return to it again! When we accept Christ, we are to break from our sinful ways ... and not return to slavery again! We are to accept Christ and be ready to run away from "Egypt" (our past life of slavery to sin) ... these two things go together! They were not allowed to eat this meal and then sit around in Egypt for a while longer! NO COMPROMISES!

"On that same night I will pass through Egypt and strike down every firstborn of both people and animals, and I will bring judgment on all the gods of Egypt. I am the Lord. [13] The blood will be a sign for you on the houses where you are, and when I see the blood, I will pass over you. No destructive plague will touch you when I strike Egypt."

— Exodus 12:12-13 —

Prophetically, just as the death angel passed over everyone that night for both Jew and Egyptian ... God's judgment will one day pass over every human who has ever lived ... and as for the Jews, only those who have applied the "blood of the Lamb" of God will be spared! This took an act of faith on the Jews' part ... to dress as though they were leaving after nine other attempts had failed. After each of the previous plagues, Pharaoh changed his mind about letting them go! Being dressed as though they were leaving demonstrated their faith that this time the blood would make the difference! This time, there would be no contest ... the defining moment had come! The blood would set them free!

Nobody Outdoes God

The gods of Egypt met more than their match in the true God of Israel ... there was no contest! Already, many of the gods of Egypt had been shown as powerless by each plague.

The Nile god "Osiris" – worshipped for giving life gave dead fish and became blood!

The frog god "Hekt" – a goddess of fertility multiplied so much that the land stank when they all died and rotted in Egypt!

The earth god "Seb" found itself struck with lice ... no match for the real God!

The god of the atmosphere "Hatkok" was struck with abundant flies.

The cattle god of Egypt "Apis" couldn't save the cows ... they were all struck with a disease ... they were no match for God!

Egypt's god "Typhon" couldn't protect them against boils ... probably leprosy and open running sores.

Egypt's god and goddess of rain and lightning

"Shu" was out of control by God's command … hail and fire raining upon Egypt destroying their crops!

Egypt's locust god "Serapia" couldn't save their crops from the hordes of locusts.

Egypt's sun god "Ra" was turned to darkness … he was no match for God here!

10 Good Reasons to Believe in God

Pharaoh and his first-born son who both were considered gods would find they, too, were no match for the God of Israel! God had given Egypt and Israel "10 Good Reasons to Believe in the True God!" Israel could trust in faith that God's salvation would work … they could dress and be ready to go, and the blood would make the difference (and still does)! Israel would not only have to believe but take action to see salvation come their way!

As long as they had the blood applied, they were safe! It served not only as a sign to God that they had faith, but it also served as a sign to each other that they had obeyed God! Nobody beats God, NOBODY! There is NO CONTEST!

Keeping the Faith Alive

Once again, Moses instructs Israel – after the fact of their deliverance – about the importance of that "door."

> *Fix these words of mine in your hearts and minds; tie them as symbols on your hands and bind them on your foreheads. [19] Teach them to your children, talking about them when you sit at home and when you walk along the road, when you lie down and when you get up. [20] Write them on the doorframes of your houses and on your gates, [21] so that your days and the days of your children may be many in the land the Lord swore to give your ancestors, as many as the days that the heavens are above the earth.*

— Deuteronomy 11:18-21 —

This time, to keep alive that faith which delivered them, they not only needed the blood applied but now they were to write God's Word on their foreheads and hands! Their forehead represented all that they think, because we use our head in thinking. Their hands represented all that they did because we work with our hands. God's Word would serve as their constant teacher throughout their life! The Word of God was to be placed everywhere in their home and in their life!

It would not be enough to just hear the priests' words about God ... each man and woman should write it on their body (their life) ... and on the door frames to their home and gate (every aspect of who they were) to remind them of God's Word!

This reveals the constant need of being reminded of God's delivering presence ... while the blood had to be applied but one time to the door frames, the Word of God is to be placed on our hearts and hands to be read over and over again! Our children need more spirituality than just what they get in church ... they need it at home, too ... written on everything that is considered our home!

Sticky Note Salvation

The theme in this passage of Scripture is that God's Word must be so common in everything around us and in us that it is a natural part of our daily life! Like the command to have it on their forehead and hands … the Word needs to literally stick to us! It should be at the entrance and exit of everything that is a part of us! This is the point of Moses' instructions! We need God's Word constantly in our lives … and so do our children! Every time Israel strayed from God, it was because they lost His Word, ignored it, or failed to teach it to the next generation!

Does Christ's Blood Cover Your Family?

Doors have two purposes: to keep things out and to let things in! A door is both an entrance and an exit. It is precisely for this reason that Israel is told to put blood on the door frames of their homes. The blood of the Lamb is to guard what comes into our homes and to sanctify what goes out!

Is Christ's blood on the door to your home and your heart?

— 2 —

Safety

Sin's nature is to ruin the family of man ... and the seeds of sin exist in all mankind! The world would like to believe Satan's lies about sin, which is "wrong is right, and right is wrong." It is thought strange to believe in sin these days or that sin is dangerous!

A Religious Fanatic's Obsession

The world has come to view the concept of sin as a religious fanatic's obsession. But, in the end, the world will come to understand just how deceiving sin is ... and how destructive it is to those who take it lightly!

One of the great dangers of our time is to think we are better than those who lived in Noah's day ... and thus we couldn't possibly be as bad as they were in warranting God's judgment on sin! Yet, consider what God is looking for. He is searching for a people who will stand up in a world controlled by sin and live a life that reflects His love and power! Anyone can follow the crowd but not everyone follows the Christ!

We Have a Door of Safety

Where are you in this world plagued with sin? God has made a way of escape from sin ... and sin's consequences, but we must enter through the door of safety!

The Bible teaches us that God has made a place of safety ... and the door is Jesus Christ! He allows us to enter into the "ark" of safety! For those who enter in, there is deliverance and life ... for those who reject it, there is only certain judgment!

The Lord saw how great the wickedness of the human race had become on the earth, and that every inclination of the thoughts of the human heart was only evil all the time. ⁶ The Lord regretted that he had made human beings on the earth, and his heart was deeply troubled. ⁷ So the Lord said, "I will wipe from the face of the earth the human race I have created— and with them the animals, the birds and the creatures that move along the ground—for I regret that I have made them." ⁸ But Noah found favor in the eyes of the Lord. ⁹ This is the account of Noah and his family.

Noah was a righteous man, blameless among the people of his time, and he walked faithfully with God. ¹⁰ Noah had three sons: Shem, Ham and Japheth.

— Genesis 6:5-7, 10 —

It was a terrible time in the earth's history. In the entire world God could only find one righteous man! Just think of that, only one righteous person in the whole world! The nations of the earth had become so corrupt that they had lost all redeeming qualities!! It was a time of prosperity and progress ... there was much pleasure to grab onto, and this led man to forget God and seek only pleasure! In the midst of all this, one man did not forget God ... his name was Noah! Though Noah surely warned them against the dangers of sin, they took no heed ... the pleasures of sin are not easily let go of!

Though God's wrath was about to come upon the earth, God does not subject His children to His wrath ... for Noah and his family, He provides a door of safety!

God Is Our Shield of Safety

Noah's escape was based on two things: God's plan and Noah's obedience! This is still true for salvation! God has provided the plan and the way. We must, however, respond in obedience!

The ark which Noah was instructed to build would shield his family from God's wrath. Inviting Jesus Christ into our lives allows Him to become our "ark of safety." In Him, like with Noah in the Ark, we are safe from God's wrath and judgment on sin! God became the necessary shelter for Noah and his family to save them from a judgment of water, and the same is true today. God is always the appropriate shelter for whatever problems or situations we face!

In Noah's day, despite the evil that had overtaken the earth, God provided a way to keep from destroying all of creation! God's provision of safety protected righteous Noah and his family ... and it also provided a way of escape for nature to survive! Why doesn't God simply destroy all the evil people today? Because His grace offers opportunity for a second chance. Yet the time is coming when the saints will board the ark of safety and be protected from the coming wrath of God. Today the door is open, just as it was for the 120 years Noah preached and yet had no converts! Today we might have questioned his credentials as a preacher ... having no converts in 120 years is not a great record of success! Most preachers today would have thrown in the towel long before reaching their 120th anniversary at a church that never grew! But ... the door remained open the whole time ... it was the door of safety for those who entered it! God does not pour out His wrath without providing a way of escape. He always offers a door of safety for those who wish to step through!

In the six hundredth year of Noah's life, on the seventeenth day of the second month—on that day all the springs of the great deep burst forth, and the floodgates of the heavens were opened. ¹² And rain fell on the earth forty days and forty nights.

¹³ On that very day Noah and his sons, Shem, Ham and Japheth, together with his wife and the wives of his three sons, entered the ark. ¹⁴ They had with them every wild animal according to its kind, all livestock according to their kinds, every creature that moves along the ground according to its kind and every bird according to its kind, everything with wings. ¹⁵ Pairs of all creatures that have the breath of life in them came to Noah and entered the ark. ¹⁶ The animals going in were male and female of every living thing, as God had commanded Noah. Then the Lord shut him in.

— Genesis 7:11-16 —

The day of wrath finally arrives ... and after a

seven-day notice, Noah and his family enter the ark along with the representatives of creation! Once inside God's provision ... they are safe from judgment!

God Controls the Door

Notice it is God who closes the door, not Noah! Like this event where God closes the door, one day God will deliver His children from His coming wrath. He will shut us in, for He is the door! God seals the door so there are no mistakes. Noah can't leave, and the undeserving can't get in! The invitation to enter was given by Noah during the previous 120 years ... now it is too late!

Nothing could deter Noah from following God's call or alter his obedience to God's will ... God's will was the most important thing on Noah's heart and mind! How many of us would have had that kind of endurance? The next time you talk about how hard it is to live like a Christian in such a sinful culture, remember the odds against Noah who lived faithfully for better than 120 years when he was literally the only one in the whole world outside his own family to serve God! The greatness of a man or woman of

God is not measured by statistics as much as by their unswerving passion to obey God! Nothing could or would keep righteous Noah from following what God asked of him ... God provided the plan and Noah provided the obedience! The result was salvation!

Did God's plan of salvation provide a life of ease for Noah and his family while sinful man was being destroyed? Of course not. There was much work to do on this great boat ... not including the seasickness which must have been a new experience for those onboard ... especially with no real windows or doors to open! As month after month passed, there was no evidence of dry land or any hope that there would be much left if land was discovered.

How well would you have coped?

Trusting God for Salvation

Noah had to be patient ... he had no idea how long this experience would last! Noah had to trust God for however long they floated and wherever they landed! And in the meantime, he had to keep happy a lot of boxed-in animals and a family that couldn't get out of each other's way! There were no servants to take care of the less-pleasant jobs ... meaning there was little free time to question God's plan!! Do you think Noah ever thought, "God, wasn't there a better way to do this that would have been more comfortable for all of us!?" How many times do we frustrate ourselves by trying to figure God out instead of simply obeying Him and trusting Him for the results?

The day finally came ... they were once again restored to the earth. Now, instead of the earth being full of evil doers, the whole world was full of only believers!

Then Noah built an altar to the Lord and, taking some of all the clean animals and clean birds, he sacrificed burnt offerings on it.

— Genesis 8:20 —

God had provided a plan of escape for them through the ark ... and not only did He provide a way to save them from His judgment, but He also provided a way for Noah to worship Him when they were free again! Remember, the animals came in by twos, all except the "clean" animals which came in by sevens! Now the reason for taking seven of every clean animal becomes very clear! The extras provided the means to worship God when they came out again on dry land without endangering the species' ability to multiply again on the earth! (God was the first one to pass a regulation to protect endangered species!) God not only provided a way to save them, but a way for them to worship appropriately!

We Are Called to Worship

God has done this for us, too … in His Son Jesus Christ! Jesus makes it possible for us to be saved! Jesus makes it possible for us to worship God, too … we come in Christ's name and in His sacrifice!

Noah was given the means to make his response to God's salvation personal! The first thing Noah did was to build an altar!! This makes our salvation very personal! Do you have an altar?

Noah's sacrifices and altar reveal his humility before God … He does not rejoice over the destruction of others; he rejoices over his own salvation. Noah doesn't walk out of the ark and say, "Guess we took care of those rotten sinners!" He understands that his own place before God is based solely on grace! Just think if he had felt he deserved to have a monument built in his honor as the only righteous man in all the earth ... perhaps a nice memorial so that others would appreciate his commitment to God ... yet, Noah builds nothing for his own honor. Rather, he builds an altar to honor God only! Noah demonstrates his humility before God through sacrificing at an altar built solely to worship God!

> *The Lord smelled the pleasing aroma and said in his heart: "Never again will I curse the ground because of humans, even though every inclination of the human heart is evil from childhood. And never again will I destroy all living creatures, as I have done. ²² As long as the earth endures, seedtime and harvest, cold and heat, summer and winter, day and night will never cease."*

— Genesis 8:21-22 —

God is pleased with this "sweet smelling sacrifice" ... there is no arrogance in Noah for being the only one saved ... just recognition of God's love and grace! Such a demonstration of humility and proper attitude prompts God's heart to promise to never again destroy the world with water! (Next time will be with fire!) God promises that everything will continue on until the end of time ... God has plans for another ark of safety better than Noah's!

The Door Is Now Open

Once again, God has provided a way of escape from His coming judgment ... and that door has been open now for 2,000 years, longer than the 120 years Noah preached while offering a time of escape! Sure enough, just as that day came after 120 years of preaching, a day is coming when the trumpet of God will sound and the door will close on the greater ark of safety! And the judgment of God will fall again on those who have failed to come aboard!

When Noah built the ark, God instructed him to build a door in it. When the time came for judgment, God shut this door! Those inside were safe, while those outside were lost! In John 10:7, Jesus referred to Himself as the "door" ... all that enter through

Christ will be safe; those outside will be lost ... forever! Have you entered the door of safety?

— 3 —

Prayer Closet

Jesus, when teaching about prayer, invites His disciples not to focus on public demonstrations of prayer but to find a place of prayer in a special "closet!"

The term "prayer closet" comes from Matthew in the King James Version of Scripture: *"But thou, when thou prayest, enter into thy closet ..."* (Matt. 6:6 KJV); but many really don't comprehend what it actually means, because they are thinking of a regular closet, not the "treasure room" which is the literal translation from the Greek word used in the original text.

So, what was Jesus trying to tell us? We are to have

a private prayer life which is an important part of our relationship with God.

But when you pray, go into your room, close the door and pray to your Father, who is unseen. Then your Father, who sees what is done in secret, will reward you.

— Matthew 6:6 —

The Greek word is "temeion" (tameion) which literally means "treasure room!" It was a secret room in every home where the family's treasures were kept for safety reasons! It was a secure room designed to guard their treasures from thieves! For this reason, it was a room usually known only to family members!

A man would enter his treasure room from time to time to be around his treasures and contemplate his wealth. For all practical purposes, it was the room where security was strongest! It is this "treasure room" that Jesus says we are to enter when we pray! The concept used in Matthew 6:21 where Jesus talks about "laying up treasures in heaven" may play into this "treasure room" idea! Today, in modern Greece, the "temeion" is the cashier in a store or office. The word translated as "closet" in some versions is still in use today but means "cashier!"

It is ironic that Jesus would choose this room to be the place for prayer ... or maybe it makes more sense than it seems! Notice that the Temple of God had a treasure room! In Nehemiah 10:38, Hezekiah got into trouble because he took allies into the treasure room in God's Temple and took pride in how much he had. Forgetting that God is our source of success and providence when surrounded by earthly treasure can be easy, unless of course we take God in there with us. Otherwise, all we will see is our "treasure." The Ethiopian Eunuch is described as the "Treasurer of Candice, Queen of Ethiopia" in Acts 8:27 ... yet, he was reflecting on God, not Candice's treasure room ... no wonder God sent Philip to talk to him! Our treasures need Christ's presence, or we will forget Him!

God wants to be invited into our "treasure room" where we can commune with Him! We should not be uncomfortable with Jesus' presence among our treasures, unless of course we have improper treasures stored there, or we are hoarding them and not sharing with God and man! If He is in our "treasure room" ... we are not nearly as likely to focus on those treasures as we are to commune with Him!

Our focus must shift from our treasures to Christ ... this is why we are told by Jesus to go into our treasure room to pray, to take the focus off our treasures and put it on Christ! In a treasure room, a man is focused on what he has, not on what he doesn't have! If he is alone in his treasure room with only his treasures, this is all he thinks about! Christ's presence in our treasure room will guard our hearts against improper attitudes toward earthly treasures!

Only God's presence can keep the situation in hand ... hence Jesus' request that we use this room to pray in rather than just focus on our earthly treasures ... to keep our attitude in check with God's presence in the very room that might lead to pride! Having Christ enter this room by prayer also helps us realize what "treasures" need to be cleared out! This is a real sign of trust to bring someone else into our treasure room ... it is the secret room, after all. To invite someone into our treasure room is a display of absolute trust in that person, for we are inviting them to share the revelation of all our treasures!

All this ties in closely with Matthew 6:19-21 and the idea of "treasure" in verse 21: *"For where your treasure is, there your heart will be also!"* In this passage, the word "treasure" relays the idea of laying up eternal things rather than earthly things. Jesus understands the connection between our heart and treasures ... that's why He wants entrance to this room!!!

> *Do not store up for yourselves treasures on earth, where moths and vermin destroy, and where thieves break in and steal. [20] But store up for yourselves treasures in heaven, where moths and vermin do not destroy, and where thieves do not break in and steal. [21] For where your treasure is, there your heart will be also.*

— Matthew 6:19-21 —

Jesus adds something new here ... move the treasure room or closet to a new location! To heaven! This way Christ can rule over it, and we can still come in prayer to visit it ... but it is safe from robbers! And since it is in heaven, we must come in a spiritual way as we enter into a spiritual realm!

He also instructs us to change the treasures we store ... from earthly things to heavenly stuff! This will preserve a "secret place" from Satan's attempts to break in and steal ... he won't find this room or our treasures because he has no access to God's dwelling place!

Having a new room for treasures and new treasures in that room will adjust our focus from an earthly one to a heavenly one. Focus is so important in our lives! This is why Jesus wanted prayer in our treasure room in the first place ... to change the focus from our treasures to Him!

Notice, too, the location changes for this room: to heaven! Now, when we want to save valuables and enter our "closet" or "treasure room" ... we go right into God's presence! Instead of us worrying about the security of all our treasures, God can watch over it all ... thus freeing us to fully commune with Him! Moving treasures to a secret place in heaven is a brilliant idea to free us to fellowship with Christ while unencumbered by fears and pride! Since our heart seems to always be focused on where our treasures are, how much more sense is it to have those treasures in heaven so that our heart stays there, too!?!

Someday, perhaps this treasure room will be included in our mansion in heaven ... still full of those treasures we put there ... and with our full communion with Christ directly in it! If both our treasures and treasure room are now in heaven, when we enter it, we come right into God's domain and Christ meets us there! Since our "heart is where our treasures are" ... we must be sure to allow Christ into this room! Now when we can enter our "prayer closet" or "treasure room" ... not only is our heart there, but we can also find the Master!

HAVE YOU ENTERED YOUR "PRAYER CLOSET" ... the "treasure room!" AND, MORE IMPORTANTLY, HAS CHRIST BEEN ALLOWED IN, TOO?

When you enter your "treasure room," are you alone, or do you invite the company of Christ to share your special time?

— 4 —

Worship

Sunday morning ... a day for those who go to church to get up, get dressed, get in the car, and head off to worship God! Sadly, that is about as much preparation for worship as the average Christian takes!

People spend more time preparing meals, or preparing for any special event, than we do for worship! But we have great expectations on what we want to receive from a church worship service!

Being Prepared

If we are not focused properly, we will miss much of what the worship experience is supposed to be about!

Like anything else, if you focus on the wrong things, you can miss the joy that is inherent in a Christ-based worship service! Many people don't enjoy church because they don't understand the reason they are there or what the church service is about.

The Bible teaches us that adequate preparation for worship is important for the experience to be all that God wants it to be! Those who put nothing into it usually get nothing out of it!

> *The Lord said to Moses, ² "Bring Aaron and his sons, their garments, the anointing oil, the bull for the sin offering, the two rams and the basket containing bread made without yeast, ³ and gather the entire assembly at the entrance to the tent of meeting."*

— Leviticus 8:1-3 —

Before Moses could ask anyone to come to the door of the tabernacle to worship God, there were certain things that needed to be done ... they had to be prepared! How could they worship without the proper items available!? Proper garments had to be rounded up ... for us, we must question whether we have on our "garment of righteousness." The anointing oil had to be brought ... it is the Holy Spirit that is our anointing oil. The sin offering had to be rounded up ... you cannot worship God unless you have accepted the sacrifice of His Son! The basket containing bread without yeast had to be in place ... the Word of God which is the "bread of life" must be included as part of your preparation to worship! And everyone had to gather at the DOOR of the Tabernacle ... both people and priests ... which tells us that corporate worship is better than worship in isolation!

Rush to Church ... or to Worship?

These are necessary items to prepare if worship is to take place when we gather with our fellow Christians! To just rush to church on Sunday morning with the sole thought of being on time with no forethought of how you will come into His presence to worship Him will leave you out of tune with God when you arrive!

*Moses did as the Lord commanded him,
and the assembly gathered at the entrance to
the tent of meeting.*

— Leviticus 8:4 —

Once the proper preparations were made ... everybody had to present themselves to the Lord at the DOOR OF THE TABERNACLE! It is foolish to prepare and then not show up, and it is equally foolish to not prepare and then show up! While only some of the priests could go further into the Holy Place under the Old Covenant, everybody could meet at the DOOR! Jesus Christ is the "DOOR" ... in Him we meet to worship together. No matter where or what the facility is, He is the DOOR!

Moses did as he was commanded ... he got everything prepared and called all Israel together to meet at the door for worship! They were all called! The people came as instructed ... obedience to come together set the stage for God's fellowship! Although some had a greater part in this service than others, they would all receive something from God!

It was not considered a "casual affair" to come into God's presence then ... and it shouldn't be now! God has never had a "casual" relationship with anybody!

Moses' first words about worship were, *"This is what the Lord has commanded to be done."* (Lev. 8:5) Worship takes preparation and participation! There were several things to take care of in getting ready to come into the presence of God ... notice the order in the following verses:

1. **The Worship Experience:** They didn't arrive and just "hope" something happened! Washing was the first order of business! The idea of "cleansing" before coming into God's presence was critical ... lest they died! (Lev. 8:6)

2. **The Clean Garment:** After their washing, a clean garment was put on! Not only must we be clean when we come to God in worship, we must be clothed with the garments of Christ's righteousness ... they must be worn! (Lev. 8:7)

3. **The Breastplate of Righteousness:** The breastplate is a part of this covering, too ... of righteousness! A covering for the head was then placed ... and on this was a gold plate that read, "Holy to the Lord"

... those who saw it became immediately aware that these priests had been separated unto God ... they belonged to the Lord! This covering was for the mind! What is written on your forehead right now? Are your thoughts "Holy to the Lord?" ... or are you drifting off mentally? (Lev. 8:8-9)

4. **The Anointing Oil:** Next was the anointing oil ... this had to be applied to the individual! The Holy Spirit must be applied to our lives for us to truly worship God! This oil was put on everything – the furnishings and the worshipper! God's Spirit is a part of the entire experience! (Lev. 8:10-13)

5. **The Sacrifice for Sin:** The sacrifice had to be a part of the process of proper worship ... here it is brought out; and Aaron and his sons lay their hands on its head as if to transfer their sins to the animal that will then die for them and their sin so that they might remain as a "living sacrifice!" Christ has already done this for us! (Lev. 8:14)

6. **The Sacrificial Blood:** Blood was then placed on the horns of the altar ... the horns were used to "bind" the sacrifice to the altar ... only the blood of Christ can attach us to the altar of God! This image was so powerful in Israel that if a man ran

to "lay hands on the horns of the altar," he could not be touched — for he had just become a "living sacrifice" by grasping the horns of the altar and creating an unbroken connection between him and God! (Lev. 8:15)

7. **We Must Offer Ourselves:** Worship is not divorced from "sacrifice" ... both the sacrifice offered on behalf of our sins and the sacrifice that we are called upon to offer (which is ourselves in the cause of Christ) are vital in our worship to God! God is pleased with the preparations and those who participate in them. It is a "sweet smelling aroma" to God! (Lev. 8:16-21)

8. **The Placement of the Blood:** Blood now was taken and some of it put on three different areas on Aaron and his sons. 1. The right lobe of Aaron's ear: so that he would always hear God's Word ... and also as the place where the awl was driven through an earlobe to signify becoming a "bond slave" ... one who gave themselves to their master for life by an act of their own will. 2. Blood was put on the thumb of the right hand ... so that his hands would only do God's work in purity! 3. Blood was also put on the big toe of the right

foot ... so that their walk would always be God-centered, that they might walk "clean" before the Lord! These three were important to participate in worship ... and they still are today! (Lev. 8:23-24)

9. **The Unleavened Bread:** Now comes the "basket of bread made without yeast" ... this was added to the sacrifice and offered up ... God's Word is very much a part of a proper worship experience ... added to the Sacrifice of God in Christ, it enables us to participate in worship properly! (Lev. 8:26-29)

10. **The Covering of the Lord's Presence:** Now again the oil is sprinkled on Aaron and his sons along with the blood, covering both their flesh and their garments! This oil, applied with the blood, brings them into God's presence in a proper way! It is not enough to talk about the Holy Spirit; He must be allowed to cover us during worship! (Lev. 8:30)

All of this was done to come into God's presence and worship Him correctly! In all these things, they had to participate to enter into worship! Worship was not a passive thing ... they didn't just sit there and expect to get hit by God's presence ... they prepared and participated! Worship requires participation on the part of the worshipper. This is true of all worship in this world!

Do you "just show up for worship" ... or do you arrive prepared and participate in worship?

God's Opinion Is the One That Counts

So Aaron and his sons did everything the Lord commanded through Moses.

— Leviticus 8:36 —

Moses did everything God told him to do ... the whole point of all this was to worship God. It didn't matter how it looked to outsiders! When we worship ... we follow God's instructions. We obey for God, not each other! It is not whether we are "pleased with the service" but, rather, whether "God is pleased with it!" The focus is on Him, not us!

It is not nearly as important how others feel about how you worship as it is how God feels about it. It doesn't even matter much how you feel about it! Worship does not happen without following God's instructions ... worship is not determined by what we like or dislike but by what pleases God!

Therefore, I urge you, brothers and sisters,
in view of God's mercy, to offer your bodies as
a living sacrifice, holy and pleasing to God—
this is your true and proper worship.

— Romans 12:1 —

Under the New Covenant, Paul introduces a fresh idea in worship ... with us being the "living sacrifices!" The only trouble with "living sacrifices," one you don't face with dead ones, is the tendency for living sacrifices to crawl off the altar! Notice that worship is a wonderfully personal thing ... we are all called to offer "our own bodies" as a living sacrifice to God! Not someone else's ... our own! We are to do so as "holy and pleasing" to God!

Offering Ourselves in Worship

It is not enough to offer our "stuff" to God ... we must offer "ourselves" too! We cannot just applaud the idea of Christianity and worship unto God; we must apply it to ourselves!

Worship is far more than just what we do on a Sunday ... we are to offer up our bodies "as living sacrifices" ... THIS IS OUR SPIRITUAL ACT OF WORSHIP! Worship is not just what we sing and what we say ... it is also what we do! Worship is not just what we do in a church facility ... it is what we do ALL the time. Worship is a personal commitment to sacrifice ourselves! When we help a friend, we are worshipping God! When we give an encouraging word ... we are worshipping God! Anything that we do with our bodies that is done for the Lord is "spiritual worship" ... and thus highly personal!

Do not conform to the pattern of this world, but be transformed by the renewing of your mind. Then you will be able to test and approve what God's will is—his good, pleasing and perfect will.

— Romans 12:2 —

This verse adds another dimension ... that worship is a process! By the "renewing of our mind," we begin "to prove what God's will is!" Since we don't learn everything all at once, this is an ongoing process! The word "transformed" in Greek is "metamorphosis" ... the process a caterpillar goes through on its way to becoming a butterfly! The renewing of our mind takes place through Word and Worship!

Becoming Like Christ

We are "no longer to be conformed to this world ... but transformed" into Christ's image! This process works well when we regularly worship and study the Word of God! Why do you go to church? What are you here to do? Who are you here for? Is there a transformation taking place in your life making you more like Christ?

The "door" of worship was where all Israel gathered to worship ... but not until proper preparations had been made ... and then the priests participated correctly. What is a proper worship experience to you? Have you truly entered the door of worship?

It is clear in the Old Testament that worship was preceded by proper preparations! When we come to worship, do we prepare properly for our entrance into God's presence as His people? The experience of worship has a direct relationship to the extent of our proper preparations! The preparations took place at the "door" of God's house ... only then did they enter into worship!

Are you prepared!?

— 5 —

Prisons

While most of us will not land in jail or experience being locked in a prison cell, there are ways that our hearts can be taken captive and our minds locked up in painful situations! These times of "prison" are difficult ... and we often wonder why God permits them. When "prison" times come, we need to be aware of the opportunities for ministry that God puts in front of us ... and to look forward to the time when the door of our prison will again be opened!

Christians Are Not Exempt from "Bad Days"

As Christians, some days will challenge us ... how

do we handle those days when everything seems to go wrong, when our emotions become "imprisoned," and we feel trapped? What do we do when things go so wrong that we find ourselves in great pain ... physically, emotionally, or spiritually?

We are not exempt from "bad days" ... but even in painful situations, we can have our prison doors opened for us by God's divine power! Our "prison" experiences are not wasted times in God's plans.

Continue Worshipping

If we wish to see our prison doors opened and discover freedom, there are steps we can take to bring that into reality ... and when done, we will find ourselves set free ... even if we are still in prison! That might sound like false hope, but God's Word says there is victory even while still in prison!

The Bible teaches us that we are to maintain our confidence in God and continue worshipping Him even when we are overwhelmed with difficult circumstances. At such times, God will do great things in our life and in the lives of others if we remain faithful!

Paul and Silas were in Philippi and found very

minimal opportunities for worship through their ministry. Evidently, the only Jewish gathering for worship was down by the river, and this was mostly attended by women! For a proper synagogue to be formed, there had to be at least ten men ... if there was not, usually a small group would meet by a water source for prayer and worship ... this is what Paul and Silas found as they entered Philippi!

God's Opportunity for Ministry

The first convert in the area was a woman named Lydia ... it's interesting that it wasn't a man who converted to Christ first! In the dream that brought Paul to Philippi, a "man from Macedonia" had called to him to "come over and help us!" (See Acts 16:9!) Yet, the fulfillment of this dream was a woman named Lydia! So much for the exact fulfillment of dreams!

Nevertheless, Paul and Silas were faithful to obey and go. To these faithful men of God, everything was an opportunity for ministry!! ... and even with such a small crowd of mostly women, they joined them for prayer.

God provides opportunities in the smallest of

situations! He has often started His work in small ways. We must be careful not to minimize God's plans based on our perceived possibility of success!

A New Opposition Arises

Once when we were going to the place of prayer, we were met by a female slave who had a spirit by which she predicted the future. She earned a great deal of money for her owners by fortune-telling.

— Acts 16:16 —

As is often the case, where God makes opportunities, the devil will raise opposition! Here, Paul and Silas are harassed by a young demon-possessed girl!

She followed Paul and the rest of us, shouting, "These men are servants of the Most High God, who are telling you the way to be saved." [18] She kept this up for many days. Finally Paul became so annoyed that he turned around and said to the spirit, "In the name of

Jesus Christ I command you to come out of her!" At that moment the spirit left her.

[19] When her owners realized that their hope of making money was gone, they seized Paul and Silas and dragged them into the market-place to face the authorities. [20] They brought them before the magistrates and said, "These men are Jews, and are throwing our city into an uproar [21] by advocating customs unlawful for us Romans to accept or practice."

— Acts:16:17-21 —

This girl had the power to predict the future, at least to some extent, and earned a profit for her owners ... the first "psychic friends' network" on record! The word used for this gift is associated with the one for "ventriloquist." Her voice must have appeared to come from somewhere else when she spoke ... giving her a sense of power that awed others! It might be that this was what she was doing as she followed Paul and Silas and called out, *"These men are servants of the Most High God, who are telling you the way to be saved!"* (Acts 16:17) She was throwing her voice as they attempted to minister!

Paul Casts Out the Demon

While what she had to say wasn't bad, Paul and Silas finally shut her down by casting the demon out of her, because they didn't want her demonic power to be associated with the Gospel! No doubt the people would have later entangled the two if she had been allowed to continue! It's interesting to consider, what if following them and calling out was also a cry from her heart to receive the salvation they preached? Then she is set free by the name of Jesus ... she has her prison door opened!

The opposition against Paul and Silas doesn't end with her deliverance, however ... in fact, it gets worse, because now a number of men who had used this girl to get rich through her so-called "gift" had lost their source of income ... the "psychic friends' network" suddenly collapsed, and with it their ability to get rich! This set the stage for a series of events that God intended to turn into opportunities for further ministry!

The truth is that being involved in ministry, even

when God is on our side, can bring opposition. We take a stand against ungodly causes, and in the conflict, we are forced to endure the heat of the opposition as they try to discredit us! The accusations against Paul and Silas claimed that they were advocating customs unlawful for the area. What this was all about was simple: Judaism was an officially recognized religion under Roman law and Christianity was not ... since these guys could not get Paul and Silas in trouble for decimating their profitable business, they instead accused them of "propagating an unapproved religion" ... for which they could be jailed!

It seems that when people lose their wealth due to the Gospel ... things start to happen. In truth, Satan often fights dirty using whatever is at hand.

Paul and Silas, however, were unruffled ... for they understood this truth: Whatever the opposition, God would provide new opportunities for ministry! This is an important concept for us to embrace if we are to overcome the prison of our emotions at times when things go against us! Paul knew to look for ways to continue his ministry even if he was restrained!

The crowd joined in the attack against Paul

and Silas, and the magistrates ordered them to
be stripped and beaten with rods. [23] *After they*
had been severely flogged, they were thrown
into prison, and the jailer was commanded to
guard them carefully. [24] *When he received*
these orders, he put them in the inner cell and
fastened their feet in the stocks.

— Acts 16:22-24 —

When the authorities realized the crowd was also angry, they tried to please them by taking Paul and Silas and having them beaten and thrown into a very rough prison! Security was usually a simple wooden beam across thick doors (the reason the doors were later open after the earthquake), but as an extra precaution, there were also stocks within the cells to hold the prisoners! These stocks were used in two ways, to secure the prisoners, and to torture them as well!

Abandoned by God?

Paul and Silas were placed in stocks after being

beaten, and no doubt they were sore, bleeding, and in great pain! At that point, most Christians would question God's love for them and why He was allowing this to happen. Weren't they ministering in the name of the Christ? Was God being unfair? Hadn't they been faithful to serve the Lord? Why would God want them to experience imprisonment and so much pain?

These are often the thoughts of those who reject God ... that God is so unfair and unjust ... but God is at work to do something truly wonderful ... and He is not indifferent to people's suffering!

Paul and Silas' ordeal was not wasted because they stayed alert to the opportunities within the opposition. God never allows things into our lives to destroy us! Within the deepest waters, God has plans to deliver us and others!

About midnight Paul and Silas were praying and singing hymns to God, and the other prisoners were listening to them. ²⁶ Suddenly there was such a violent earthquake that the foundations of the prison were shaken. At once all the prison doors flew open, and *everyone's chains came loose.* ²⁷ *The jailer woke up, and when he saw the prison doors open, he drew his sword and was about to kill himself because he thought the prisoners had escaped.* ²⁸ *But Paul shouted, "Don't harm yourself! We are all here!"*

— Acts 16:25-28 —

What did Paul and Silas do in their seemingly hopeless situation? Despite their pain and confusion, they began to worship God! Notice that as they sang, the other prisoners listened to the hymns and praise choruses! Even trapped in stocks and suffering, they were preaching. Paul and Silas found a way to minister even through their pain!

At such times in our lives ... what do we do? Do we act defeated ... become angry with God and others? Do we pull away from God and from the church? Paul had one objective in his life ... to glorify God in EVERYTHING! Though in pain, tired, abused, etc., he found that his heart was not imprisoned! Silas also joined him in worship!

Worship Is Our Key to Spiritual Freedom

Paul and Silas didn't question God's will and His goodness ... there was no "Why me, Lord?" ... just worship! Though Satan was trying to crush Paul and Silas' ministry, the "crushing" was only bringing out the "sweetest fruit" in their lives.

How are you handling "tribulation" that has come into your life ... are you singing worship hymns at midnight ... or tossing all night in pain and anger?

During Paul and Silas's new prison worship ministry, a great earthquake hit and opened the prison doors! Paul and Silas were already free in their hearts, but God knew how to really set them free! Even so, with the doors of the prison open, Paul and Silas didn't leave! They knew that any guard that lost a prisoner ... no matter the reason ... would be put to death by Roman law! Their freedom would cost the life of the man who guarded them! Paul could not enjoy his freedom at the expense of another man's life!

We Are All Here!

So, as the jailer was preparing to end his own life

quickly rather than suffer the humility of the Roman system putting him to death, Paul and Silas call out that they are all there … including the other prisoners! Why didn't the others leave? Perhaps they were too amazed at Paul and Silas's testimony, revealed through worshiping even when they were in pain, to want to go; or perhaps they wanted to know what these men had that they didn't have! In any case, they surely realized they were in the company of men who knew God! They didn't want to go … they were taken "captive" by Paul and Silas' example of worship!

Paul's objective in life was never his own freedom … but the freedom of those imprisoned by sin! The door of the prison was open … but freedom needed to come for others before he would walk out!

The jailer called for lights, rushed in and fell trembling before Paul and Silas. ³⁰ He then brought them out and asked, "Sirs, what must I do to be saved?"

³¹ They replied, "Believe in the Lord Jesus, and you will be saved—you and your household." ³² Then they spoke the word of the Lord to him and to all the others in his house. *³³ At that hour of the night the jailer took them and washed their wounds; then immediately he and all his household were baptized. ³⁴ The jailer brought them into his house and set a meal before them; he was filled with joy because he had come to believe in God—he and his whole household.*

— Acts 16:29-34 —

While most Christians would have seen the open door as an opportunity to get free while not worrying about anyone else ... Paul stayed to minister to this man and his family! The jailer fell trembling before Paul and Silas and asked, "What must I do to be saved?" When our lives truly reflect the fact that we have died to self and are here to serve others and Christ, people will come to us and want to be saved! We must never underestimate the power of our witness!

The jailer becomes a believer as do all within his household ... and they are all baptized! Since those in the household "believed," they could not have been infants! His entire family of adults accepts Christ as

Lord!

Paul and Silas' prison experience was used by God to set others free! They were not interested in their own physical freedom as much as the freedom from sin others might gain!

God Opens the Doors a Second Time

Ironically, even when God opened the prison doors and Paul and Silas could leave, they returned of their own free will! The next morning, God opened the doors of the prison a second time when the magistrates sent a message that the two men of God could officially be set free! This second time, however, everyone was free ... including the jailer!

Imagine the joy in this jailer as he witnessed God's miracle in setting these men free again ... a second time the door of the prison opened for them, this time in a legal way that left no one punished! This time they were free to go, as their work here was done! Their suffering had resulted in another man's salvation, along with his family!

Protecting the Church in Philippi

Paul, however, had one more obligation to take care of ... the church in Philippi! He demanded that the authorities come personally and apologize to him and Silas and escort them publicly out of town! Why did Paul do this? Was he trying to get even? NO! It was forbidden to flog a Roman citizen ... even one found guilty in a court of law! To do so could result in serious punishment for the officials who had ordered it! Paul and Silas were both Roman citizens and had not even had a trial in Philippi before they were flogged! Paul probably knew that if they were punished, the authorities would likely go after the other believers in town ... UNLESS they were afraid to do so! By using his Roman citizenship, he puts fear in the authorities, for he could get them into serious trouble for what they did to him and Silas ... no doubt Paul wanted a public apology so that they would think twice in the future about trying to go after the church in Philippi whom Paul had helped oversee! Paul was once again not thinking of himself (even though it might seem so to some) but was thinking about the church's safety after he left!

Paul recognized his obligations before God ... no

matter the pain, to worship; no matter the freedom, to lead people to Christ; no matter the personal injury, to minister to others and protect the church! For Paul, the prison doors had always been open ... even before they were opened by God's earthquake!

Victory Through Worship

How about your prison doors? The secret to escaping from your prison ... especially emotional and spiritual imprisonment ... is to do as Paul and Silas and discover freedom even in your prison. Paul and Silas were never imprisoned in their minds ... they lived in victory no matter the circumstances! Their example is your guide to open the locked door of your prison!

Will you choose to find your freedom through worshipping God?

— 6 —

Death

Have you ever noticed how we avoid the subject of death? Americans, like no others, do everything we can to avoid facing it or talking about it! We have youth serums and creams; and we take injections to remove wrinkles from our faces to avoid the appearance of age. We reach for everything we can to avoid the reality of death or even thinking about its impending arrival. We strive to look good up until we die ... but the reality is that we will still die!

We live as though we will never die ... but death is certain! Death to a Christian should be viewed in an entirely different way than the world views death. To the world, the door of death is the thing they dread most; to the Christian, death is the door to life!

Christ's Resurrection Is Key

Christianity without the resurrection isn't Christianity!! We serve a God that has power over life and death! As His followers, the door of death holds no terror! Jesus is the "resurrection and the life!"

The Bible teaches us that Jesus is "the life" ... that He has conquered death, and those who have faith in His saving work need not fear the door of death! Christ has power over death!

Despair usually strikes Christians both after great losses and great successes! Remember Elijah ... after beating the 450 prophets of Baal, he was a great success, yet he ran away from Jezebel who had threatened to take his life. He became severely depressed! We know this because he showed all the classic symptoms of depression: going days without sleep; isolating himself in the desert; and leaving behind his helper. He also eats poorly, ignores God's Word; and assumes the worst about God.

During his depression, Elijah saw no future for himself. He sought no counsel from friends. He believed that what he did wouldn't have any lasting impact. He assumed he was the only one living for God properly!

Lazarus, Good and Dead

With worry also comes blame!

Martha and Mary suffered a great loss when they lost their brother Lazarus ... all of whom were especially close friends with Jesus! They had probably helped finance much of Jesus' ministry. Their house was a frequent stop for Jesus.

Yet, despite their intimate connection, in their deepest hour of need, Jesus was not there to minister to them, and despair set in! On top of this, Jesus deliberately stayed away long enough to ensure that Lazarus was good and dead!

Imagine how this felt to Martha and Mary ... they had sent word to Jesus *before* Lazarus died ... and Jesus didn't come! To His disciples, Jesus explained that Lazarus was only "sleeping," creating greater confusion when they got the wrong idea and thought Lazarus was recovering from an illness.

When Jesus explained that He meant he had died,

the disciples also fell into despair ... especially when Jesus explained that they were going back to Bethany now that Lazarus was dead. Thomas assumed this meant they were all going to die ... and so he was ready! (John 11:16)

The True Nature of Jesus

Death brings out profound despair in people! Martha and Mary imply that Jesus is somewhat to blame ... if He had been there, this wouldn't have happened. (They both state this outright, Martha in John 11:21a; and Mary in John 11:32b.) It seems quite clear that neither Martha nor Mary (nor the disciples) really understood the nature of Jesus' life and power! They could believe for healing if Jesus was present ... and maybe at a stretch, like many of the others Jesus had raised from the dead, He could have brought back Lazarus immediately after death ... but a man dead four days already ... that was something else!

Even when Jesus explained that Lazarus would be raised, they didn't think in terms of "now" ... only sometime in the future! Yet, Jesus is THE LIFE ...

HE IS THE RESURRECTION POWER! Death cannot exist in the presence of Jesus ... His life gives power! Notice in the Gospels that at EVERY funeral Jesus is recorded as attending, the dead person comes back to life!

Despair was everywhere, both in Martha's and Mary's heart and in the hearts of the mourners that were present. The mourners usually stayed seven days to mourn with the family ... the reason we find them still there four days after Lazarus' death. However, Jesus is the power of life! The door of death is nothing in the presence of the giver of life! They are all weeping over death ... *oh, if only Jesus had been there earlier!* Yet, Jesus' lateness was no accident! He intended to teach them that no barrier is too great for God!

Jesus Sees Our Anguish

Notice that Jesus even wept in sorrow! The phrase, "He was deeply moved in spirit and troubled," is interesting. In the Greek it means, "He was enraged in spirit and troubled himself!" Jesus' response to Lazarus' death was a mixture of both tears and anger!

The tears were for the anguish that death brings to humanity! After all ... this was not God's original plan for man! The anger was no doubt over the pain that death brings to His creation, for death brings indignity to humanity.

The people whom Jesus loved so deeply didn't fully understand the nature of His power or life, leaving them misguided in their despair! Jesus knew this, and He was broken over their despair and inability to see His power!

Remove the Door!

Jesus then moved toward the tomb like a gladiator ready to do battle ... like a champion! The first thing He asked was to have the DOOR TO THE DEAD removed! There must be no barrier between Jesus and us! Why were they sorrowing ... wasn't He there ... hadn't He already shown that He had the power over life and death!?

The barrier between our Lord and Lazarus ... it must be removed! This stone door was a symbol of their despair ... there was no longer any hope in their heart for Jesus to do something ... the door had been placed!

Like many today, they felt that death was the final loss. However, their despair was misplaced ... didn't they know that they were on the winning team? They needn't despair!

Lost Hope Restored

Martha and Mary's problem was that they had lost hope! And the loss of hope brings despair! Hope is a powerful force ... if we ever lose it, we lose everything ... but with it comes strength! If Martha and Mary could have maintained their hope in Christ ... even against Lazarus' recent death ... how much easier their lives would have been. Jesus knew that their hope needed restoration! The first step was to remove the stone barrier preventing Him from going to Lazarus. For us, it is getting rid of our heart of stone ... rolling aside whatever emotional or relational barrier we face that prevents us from finding hope in Christ!

Imagine what must have been going on in Martha and Mary's minds (and the rest of those around the tomb) when they heard Jesus declare in a loud voice: "Lazarus, come forth!" Martha, the practical sister, had informed Jesus that Lazarus was already dead for four days, and that he would surely stink! Isn't it nice to have practical people around to tell you what God can't do ... even to keep God updated on what He might have missed and needs to know?

How many times had they seen Jesus do the impossible ... but somehow, this seemed more impossible!?

How do we limit God? How big is your God?

Doubt Turns to Faith

What must have run through their minds when Lazarus shuffled through the entrance of the tomb still wrapped in smelly grave clothes? Suddenly, doubt turned to faith! Jesus was now viewed differently ... "He is the resurrection and the life!"

Death has a way of fleeing from Christ ... in His presence, death can't stick around! Not even the grave can hold Jesus, for He is life! That is why in heaven we won't die! We will be in Christ's presence for all time, so we will live eternally!

We Have a Part to Play

There was still a job to be done by Lazarus' family and friends, though ... they were asked by Jesus to unwrap him! After all, Lazarus' family and friends were the ones who had put the grave clothes on him! While Jesus gave Lazarus back his life ... Lazarus' family and friends must help the man out of his grave clothes!

This is still our job in the family of God ... when Christ saves someone and they receive a new life in Him, the family of God is called upon to help them remove the smell of death from their life! We are to help unwrap their new life in Christ from their old clothes of death! Since Christ has conquered death and given life to those who believe on Him, we are called upon to minister to them, to help unwrap them from the cold death of sin, to remove the bondages (bandages!) from their lives! Jesus commands them to "take off the grave clothes and let him go!"

This command still holds for us today! Are we helping people out of their grave clothes? What happens when we do? Many people believe! And many people don't believe, as well! In the case of Lazarus, they ran to the authorities to get Jesus in trouble!

The Jews Feel Threatened

The Jews felt threatened by this miracle ... instead of rejoicing over it, they were more concerned about their personal lifestyle and position not being interrupted! There are those today who still don't want to consider the claims of Christ ... they don't want to think about eternal life and death. It only upsets their way of living!

Yet, Jesus cannot be ignored. What will it be ... will you choose to believe?

Jesus' Coming Is Real

Do you believe He is coming again? Not even the dead will stay in their graves! Jesus' coming is real ... and so is His power, even if we try and ignore it!

How are you dealing with the door of death?

The most formidable door that humans face is the door of death! Throughout history, no man has been able to break down this door ... except one! All religions have the graves of their founders, and inside them lay the bodies of men ... but one grave is empty, the grave of Jesus outside of Jerusalem! He is the "Resurrection and the Life," and if we believe in Him, we too will never die!

— 7 —

Faithfulness

Faithfulness is not so much a product as it is a process! Being faithful to God this week doesn't guarantee that you will not have to discipline yourself to be faithful to Him next week! Faithfulness requires an act of will ... all the time! We must continuously choose to be faithful to the Lord. Even living faithfully for many years doesn't prevent us from letting down our guard for a moment and falling into the trap of unfaithfulness!

Faithfulness is not a product of feelings but an act of our will! If we live by our feelings, we will endure a life of on-and-off faithfulness! Those who let their emotions rule their lives find ways to excuse their lack of faithfulness rather than deal with it!

The Core of Our Faith

Faithfulness is at the very core of Christianity ... and not a lukewarm commitment, either! We focus too much sometimes on God's faithfulness and not enough on our own ... we like messages about God's faithfulness to us, but since this is never in doubt, we need more preaching about our faithfulness to Him!

The door of faithfulness begins with our will once we accept Christ as our Lord! We have built a billion-dollar industry in America to get in touch with our feelings and emotions, to understand WHY we do things instead of learning to serve faithfully and make correct decisions! Our heart will catch up with our will when we apply ourselves to always being faithful!

Busy at the Lord's Work

The Bible teaches us that we are to guard our lives against unfaithfulness, that we are to be busy in doing our Lord's work and His will, not our own!

In the spring, at the time when kings go off to war, David sent Joab out with the king's men and the whole Israelite army. They destroyed the Ammonites and besieged Rabbah. But David remained in Jerusalem.

² One evening David got up from his bed and walked around on the roof of the palace. From the roof he saw a woman bathing. The woman was very beautiful, ³ and David sent someone to find out about her. The man said, "She is Bathsheba, the daughter of Eliam and the wife of Uriah the Hittite." ⁴ Then David sent messengers to get her. She came to him, and he slept with her. (Now she was purifying herself from her monthly uncleanness.) Then she went back home. ⁵ The woman conceived and sent word to David, saying, "I am pregnant."

— 2 Samuel 11:1-5 —

In antiquity, wars and fighting were reserved for the good weather months. Often, everyone took off from fighting during winter ... but come spring, it was time for the kings to go out and fight the enemy again! It was such a time in this passage ... the time for the kings to ready their men and go off to war against the enemy!

David Chooses Not to Fight

We are told that David chose not to go with his troops but sent Joab, instead ... a very unusual situation for a king in Israel! We can only speculate as to the reason. Many pagan kings stayed in their luxurious palaces while their men went off to war, but Israel's kings were not to be like the pagan kings. They were to be "servant-leaders" and lead their men in the fight! Saul had fought alongside his men when he was king! David had also gone into battle ... he was known as a great warrior!

David detaching himself from his brethren to not go and fight the enemy was not a good sign!

As David grew older, maybe he thought he could take it easy and enjoy his previous victories ... a situation that always leaves us open to temptation! He may have thought it was time for the younger ones to do more! He may have thought that he should be allowed to enjoy the fruits of his earlier sacrifices! He may have even justified staying behind so that Jerusalem had leadership present and ready to respond to any crisis!

Tragically, most people who fell in the Bible did so later in their lives, not in their youth! No matter how good the reasons might have been ... when the enemy was attacking, David should have been in the battle! There was no excuse to be idle!

Even if you're on the right track, you'll get run over if you just sit there!!!

An Afternoon Nap Goes Sideways

Detached from his fighting men, David indulged in an afternoon siesta and woke toward evening with nothing to do! Isolation has always been a favorite tool of Satan to get us to stumble!!! Alone, we can fall much more easily! Such was Satan's ploy with Eve!

The Word states, "One evening David got up from his bed." (2 Sam. 11:2a) His men were on the war front putting their lives on the line, while he was walking back and forth with nothing to do! David grew bored, so he headed to his palace roof to "walk around." The Hebrew verb indicates a "pacing back and forth while getting nowhere." The adage, "an idle mind is the devil's workshop," was about to become reality for David! As he gazed below, he noticed a very beautiful woman by the name of Bathsheba bathing.

In David's boredom, lust took root!

Lust Rears Its Head

What began with a GLANCE ended with a GAZE ... and turned into lust in David's heart!

David, who wrote so often how he delighted in the Laws of God, allowed himself to become distracted away from those same laws! While he might not have been able to help the quick glance, he didn't have to continue to gaze upon her! Physical passion was now in place. He already had several wives he could have turned to ... but he wanted what he didn't have! This is the passion of sin ... to take what is not rightfully ours!

The king who should have been FIGHTING the enemy was now FLIRTING with the real enemy! Flirting will usually lead to FAILURE! He called for his servants to find out who this beautiful woman was! They informed David that she was a married woman, the wife of one of his finest soldiers, a non-Jew, a Hittite named Uriah ... perhaps David justified his interests in her since her husband wasn't one of God's covenant people!

The man who had a "heart after God's own heart" allowed these distractions to pull his heart away from God and God's Word! Had he been faithfully serving with his brethren, this would not have happened! It is clear in Scripture that Bathsheba became pregnant with David's child ... this is made sure by the insertion in the fourth verse that "she had just purified herself from her uncleanness." This was a reference to having just finished her monthly cycle and having made herself clean by the law ... thus she could not have been pregnant before they slept together!

The Consequence of David's Sin

Bathsheba slept with David, and the result of this adulterous affair was a pregnancy!

David should have put her out of his heart the moment he saw her ... by focusing on her, he became distracted from what he knew to be right, thus he sinned! We must learn to clear out the distractions in our lives lest they lead us into sin! A man who is not serving God on the front lines is a good candidate to become distracted ... and to fail!

So David sent this word to Joab: "Send me Uriah the Hittite." And Joab sent him to David. ⁷ When Uriah came to him, David asked him how Joab was, how the soldiers were and how the war was going. ⁸ Then David said to Uriah, "Go down to your house and wash your feet." So Uriah left the palace, and a gift from the king was sent after him. ⁹ But Uriah slept at the entrance to the palace with all his master's servants and did not go down to his house.

¹⁰ David was told, "Uriah did not go home." So he asked Uriah, "Haven't you just come from a military campaign? Why didn't you go home?"

¹¹ Uriah said to David, "The ark and Israel and Judah are staying in tents, and my commander Joab and my lord's men are camped in the open country. How could I go to my house to eat and drink and make love to

my wife? As surely as you live, I will not do
such a thing!"

— 2 Samuel 11:6-11 —

David asked his commander on the front lines to
send Uriah back to him ... he hoped to cover up his
sin rather than confess it! This was a terrible mistake
... the only way to deal with sin is to repent of it! The
extent that David intended to go through to cover up
his sin was far greater than the effort it would have
taken to simply confess his sin!

From Adultery to Murder

It was bad enough that David sinned by com-
mitting adultery, but then he conspired to commit
murder!! One sin has a way of leading to other, greater
sins if left unconfessed! We cannot strip sin of its
power over us by our own wit and strength!

Uriah the Hittite arrived, and David indulged in
"small talk" ... "How's Joab doing ..." (2 Sam. 11:7a);
"How's the soldiers doing ..." (2 Sam. 11:7b); and
"How's the war going ..." (2 Sam. 11:7c).

The fact that no responses are recorded by Uriah suggests that David wasn't listening to what he said, anyway! David was bent on justifying himself and protecting himself ... he had no concern for what his men were going through, and that included Uriah!

David asked Uriah to go home to his wife and even sent along gifts to make the night a wonderfully romantic evening for the two of them!!! (2 Sam. 11:8) This was not the generous offer of a king, however. David was hoping to get Uriah romantically involved with his wife in the hopes that her current pregnancy (by David) would be covered up.

A Man of Character and Faithfulness

David was "using" Uriah by being overly generous to him! Uriah didn't go home, however!!!! (2 Sam. 11:9) Though not a Jew, Uriah showed himself a man of character and faithfulness! It must have blown David out of the water to find Uriah at his own door the next morning ... sleeping on a mat with the other servants! David asked him why he didn't go home to his wife ... and Uriah's answer reveals a man of deep faithfulness.

Uriah's first reason why he wouldn't take pleasure for himself had to do with the "Ark of the Covenant" being in the field where God's people were fighting (2 Sam. 11:11a) ... Uriah could not think of pleasure when God's presence was being contested by enemies. He put the Lord first as his reason for self-sacrifice and denial of personal pleasures ... and this was a non-covenant born man! A faithful man puts God first ... always! The second reason he gave: "Israel and Judah are staying in tents." (2 Sam. 11:11b) He would not take liberties his brothers could not have ... he chose to live as they do! The third reason: "and my Lord's men" (also in 2 Sam. 11:11b) ... recognized David's leadership and respected the task assigned him by the king ... which was not yet finished! Work first, play later!

Uriah was emphatic about the cost of faithfulness ... he would not take his own freedoms when there was a job to do ... no matter his own part, he would serve God first and then others! For Uriah, faithfulness was not based on how glamorous the job was, nor how difficult ... but on how faithful he was to do what had been given to him! There is no hint that he sought a prestigious position; he didn't make excuses that he shouldn't have to serve ... he could have claimed his right not to serve. After all, he wasn't even Jewish; he was a Hittite! Faithfulness was an absolute for Uriah ... how about us?

David Faces Frustration Once More

David tried one more time ... this time he invited Uriah to dinner night at the palace, and David got Uriah drunk! (2 Sam. 11:12-13) David figured the man had too much character to sin ... so he attempted to drug him up and lower that quality in his life! David was determined to take care of his own sin by covering it up! And Uriah was determined to be faithful to God no matter what!

Who do you think will win?

To David's utter shock, the next morning he again discovered Uriah sleeping at his doorstep with the other servants ... he was too devoted to serving God, God's people, and the king to be unfaithful! Uriah was a man of unwavering faithfulness ... he made up his mind and that was that. Even in a stupor he would not yield to distraction! This sure put the Jewish King David's example to shame! Uriah set his course ... and he would not be sidetracked!

Can we say the same today about our walk with God? God's people need to learn to say "no" to sin and mean it. Rather than try and analyze our feelings of why we are drawn to sin, we should learn from others' failures and "just say no!" Uriah could have easily justified going home and having some fun ... he had been fighting hard already! He was asked to return home by the king! He wasn't a Jew, anyway!

Uriah, however, was too focused on being faithful; and he would allow no distractions from his perceived duty. He knew his duty ... and he was determined to do it ... no matter what! This demonstrates the properties of faithfulness!

Joab sent David a full account of the battle. ¹⁹ *He instructed the messenger: "When you have finished giving the king this account of the battle,* ²⁰ *the king's anger may flare up, and he may ask you, 'Why did you get so close to the city to fight? Didn't you know they would shoot arrows from the wall?* ²¹ *Who killed Abimelek son of Jerub-Besheth? Didn't a woman drop an upper millstone on him from*

the wall, so that he died in Thebez? Why did
you get so close to the wall?' If he asks you this,
then say to him, 'Moreover, your servant Uriah
the Hittite is dead.'"

— 2 Samuel 11:18-21 —

David had sent a message back to have Uriah put
in the front lines where the battle was the hottest to
ensure Uriah would be killed! He not only planned
Uriah's murder ... he had Uriah carry the message back
to Joab that would end in his own death! Uriah was
so trustworthy and faithful that David could trust him
to not read the message that would send him to his
own death!

David Gets What He Wants

Not was Uriah killed, but to get him to the front
lines, Joab sent others with him so it didn't look too
obvious ... and so others lost their lives, too ... something that Joab tried to pin on David with the message
he sent back! (2 Sam. 11:18-21)

David received the message that several had died

... and instead of getting angry like Joab thought he might, that other innocent lives were lost, David was not even moved over the losses, just relieved that Uriah was dead! Joab assumed David would question letting the men get so close to the wall where they were easy targets ... but David's value of life had diminished as he covered his sin.

Sin in our land is a reproach to the values of life! The truth could have set David free ... but instead he was still in bondage!

A Sheep from a Poor Man

David had demeaned human life, the dignity of being the king of Israel, and God's laws all because he desired to cover up his sin! This so affected his perspective that he took no pity on the losses of his own men fighting for him and Israel! He took delight only in getting rid of Uriah!

David was not even moved over the death of several of his men along with Uriah ... he had lost his compassion! Covering his sin was hardening his heart ... it was searing his conscience!

David could see others' faults, but not his own!

This becomes evident in the next chapter when Nathan tells him the parable of the man who took a sheep from a poor man ... David becomes outraged over this, but not over his own sins of adultery and murder! The loss of feelings comes when we harden our heart against God! Sin makes us emotionally crippled ... the truly best way to mental health is confession of sin to God and the forgiveness that results from it! The king who was supposed to lead his men, to fight for them, to take care of others, could only see his own needs ... he was cold to the needs of others!

Faithfulness Is a Choice

The door to faithfulness opens through our will ... will we serve God wholeheartedly? Will we confess our sins when we commit them or just hide them? Will we live by God's laws no matter what this world tells us!? Will we remain faithful, no matter how we feel at any moment?

No one drowns from just falling into the water; they drown by staying in the water!

Faithfulness does not come by default ... it comes by design! The door is our will! David's poor choices led him into unfaithfulness, yet a non-Jew by the name of Uriah made wise choices that honored God, God's people, and God's leaders!

Which example are you following?

— 8 —

Opportunities

We live in a time when everyone is interested in security. We are so security-minded that we are reluctant to take risks or seek out new opportunities! Being a Christian always carries a level of risk as it goes against the status quo! It means living a disciplined life in an age of "just let it all go!" It means being committed to values that are on their way out! It means putting character above cash ... and family above fortune!

Witnessing to others is risky; it means being labeled ... perhaps even persecuted by others.

The early church understood the risks far greater than we do today, yet they took those risks. They seized the opportunities open to them and so must we. God opens creative doors for us to use ... we must recognize the doors of opportunity and step through them!

Responding to God's Opportunities

The Bible teaches us that we are to utilize God-given opportunities He makes available to us so that we can do His good works! It is not necessarily the largest church that has the most strength; it is the faithful church that responds that finds God's strength!

To the angel of the church in Philadelphia write: These are the words of him who is holy and true, who holds the key of David. What he opens no one can shut, and what he shuts no one can open.

— Revelation 3:7 —

The message opens by affirming God's control over everything ... even the opportunities that come our way! *"Him who is holy and true"* ... Jesus! *"Who holds the key of David"* ... the King of the Kingdom!

Then we read the uplifting truth the writer wants to convey: *"What He opens, no one can shut, and what He shuts, no one can open!"*

No Opportunity Is Too Small

Christ is in control! When God opens doors, there is nothing the enemy can do to close them, and when He closes them, the enemy is helpless in trying to open them! In a major city like ancient Philadelphia, a city big on business opportunities due to major trade routes through the city, this was an important concept!

Being a small, insignificant church, with little money or power (referenced later by a comment about their "little strength"), this church needed to grasp this core concept: God could open and close doors for them ... and nothing could work against that! They needed to know that size, money, and power were not the most important factors when seeking to do something for God!

How many missed opportunities from God have

come and gone because we failed to see properly what God might be able to do? "What difference will it make?" "They never were interested before!" "They have their own ideas!" "It is such a small thing ... it won't have any effect, anyway!"

I know your deeds. See, I have placed before you an open door that no one can shut. I know that you have little strength, yet you have kept my word and have not denied my name.

— Revelation 3:8 —

God knew about their deeds despite their small size! Though they were a small and insignificant church ... they were not lazy or inactive ... they were willing to work for God! Because of their willingness to do what they could do ... God would place "open doors" (opportunities) ... before them! For those willing to be used by God, there will always be opportunities!

The formula here is interesting: Work first ... and then expect opportunities! Too many times we wait for a big opportunity before we consider working! The verse starts with recognizing their deeds ... then promises more open doors! This church was small ... but they had done two things correctly! *"Yet you have kept my Word ..." "And have not denied my Name!"*

They were not reticent about their faith and the message of salvation! It did not matter that they were small ... obedience was what mattered! No work they did was considered insignificant! This message from God must have inspired confidence in this small church! And it should in us, too!

I will make those who are of the synagogue of Satan, who claim to be Jews though they are not, but are liars—I will make them come and fall down at your feet and acknowledge that I have loved you.

— Revelation 3:9 —

The church that does nothing is no threat ... no matter how big it is! This small church had taken the opportunities God had given it ... and this had stirred up a reaction against them! Satan is not threatened by a comfortable church ... only a committed church! Though small, the church in Philadelphia was active in sharing the message ... they did not consider their size or strength a restriction of "doing deeds." In this church, there were few if any that sat on the sidelines hoping something got done!

Challenges Now ... Rewards to Come

The church that is seizing the opportunities that God gives it is a church that will be challenged by the enemy! God promised the church in Philadelphia that one day their challengers would fall at their feet and admit that God loves them! While the pressures might come now ... the rewards will come later to those who are engaged in the battle for the souls of men and women!

An active church should not be surprised by conflicts that come its way. For the Philadelphians, most of the conflict was from religious people! Often the enemy seeks to destroy God's work from the inside! The danger comes when those in the church decide they no longer want to be challenged ... they choose to give up God's work and the opportunities

He provides in exchange for temporary peace and quiet!

Since you have kept my command to endure patiently, I will also keep you from the hour of trial that is going to come on the whole world to test the inhabitants of the earth.

— Revelation 3:10 —

The word "since" indicates a conclusion ... since they had remained faithful despite challenges and persecution, because they had ENDURED FAITH-FULLY and not given up on God's opportunities, God offered a promise of reward for them: He would keep them from the hour of trial that was coming on the whole earth! They would be unmoved when the rest of the world faced the real test, for it was a test they had already passed! God would confine their struggle to something manageable ... they would not be overwhelmed! The original Greek for the word "from" is "ek" which can be translated either "out of" or "through" and could mean the rapture before the tribulation or after ... but the main point is clear: God will spare those who are faithful!

God puts limits on what comes against a faithful church or believer. Satan does not have free reign over the saints of God! The promise of God's reward was given to the church at Philadelphia because they had "faithfully endured." They had been patient ... a lost quality of Christianity today ... today we want everything immediately ... we need to learn to be patient! We need to learn to patiently endure right up to the end ... even when it seems there is no way to win!

God has the final move in history ... and to those who patiently endure, we will win! Satan's power and plans are confined by God ... and so is the pressure Satan can put on God's people!

[11] I am coming soon. Hold on to what you have, so that no one will take your crown.
[20] Here I am! I stand at the door and knock. If anyone hears my voice and opens the door, I will come in and eat with that person, and they with me.

— Revelation 3:11, 20 —

The message concludes with several important statements from God intended both to encourage us to endure and to act! "He is coming!" The opportunities and the opposition have limited possibilities! "Hold on to what you have!" Don't give up! Don't ignore the basics!

No Social-Club Commitments Allowed

Technically, no one can take our crown ... but we can forfeit it by lack of action! It is clear this is a reference to rewards! The danger of the church is to pull back and relax when things are either going well or the pressure seems too tough! The *"hold on to what you have"* is a call for the church to not lose sight of what it exists for ... to save the lost ... lest we lose the rewards of winning the lost! "Church" must not become just a social club or institution where we come to get peace of mind! It is a place where we receive so that we might go forth to give!

The fact that Jesus is coming soon should inspire us to a deeper commitment ... to do what can be done while it can be done! We have learned to recognize economic opportunities ... to seize them when they come ... what about spiritual ones!? As followers of Christ, we will be spared the trial revealed in Revelation that is coming upon the earth ... however, many that we know will not be ... we need to reach them now while it is still day!

A Pillar of the Church

For now, Christ is standing at the door knocking! (Rev. 3:20) This may well be the door to the church! After all, this verse is written to the church, telling us that Jesus is knocking on the door!! Perhaps Christ is on the outside trying to get back in. Importantly, we must remember that this won't always be true!

Are you prepared to open the door?

Him who overcomes I will make a pillar in the temple of my God.

— Revelation 3:12 —

Earthquakes were well-known to the people of Philadelphia. Yet, even when the frequent earthquakes leveled temples ... the pillars were left standing! This was a familiar sight to the citizens of Philadelphia ... these pillars were a symbol of durability ... and God used that symbol to assure them that they would be like those pillars in the temple of God ... still standing after all the shaking! The church at Philadelphia would endure even after facing many trials.

Much like the enduring pillars around the city of Philadelphia still standing after an earthquake, God's promise here is clear ... He commends those who "stay the course" faithfully ... they will remain unbroken by all that comes upon mankind!

God's Own

God also promises them a "new name." We will be given God's own name ... for we will reflect the very character of God by our faithful service! In antiquity, to be given the name of the emperor was a very special privilege! It gave you the rights to all that he had ... and gave you a place of prominence! This promise of a "new name" was akin to being given all that belongs to God ... making available to us all that is His! What a privilege for the faithful saint or church!

Those that are commended by God will have a

great reward: *"He that hath an ear let him hear what the Spirit says to the churches!"* (Rev. 2:7) The church is, after all, us, not buildings! What is the Spirit saying to you? Have you been faithful to the door of opportunity ... or are you just content to wear your football jersey to the morning service?

Opportunities for ministry are not determined by a church's size, money, power, or programs! They are determined by God! God gives opportunities to minister to every church and every believer, but we must "seize the day!" God may open the door, but we must walk through it! Success requires two things:

1. See the opportunity.

2. Act on the opportunity.

Do you see possibilities for you to minister? What are you doing about it?

A Final Word

You can find Tim on the South Texas District website at www.stxag.org, on Facebook, or at his Houston office when he's not traveling his home state ministering in the churches across the South Texas District.

He'd be thrilled to connect with you and share stories of God's faithfulness.

Additional Books by
Tim R. Barker

If you liked this book, you may be interested in additional books Tim has written. Turn the page for a short description of each book. All are available on Amazon.

My *Jesus* Journey

This soul-building, introspective 4-book series reveals Tim's innermost heart on subjects that affect all of us, from Cooperation to Loyalty to The Truth of Salvation and more.

The books in this series include:

My Jesus Journey
My Jesus Journey: Crescendo
My Jesus Journey: Glissando
My Jesus Journey: Rhapsody

At *Your* Feet

In this book, you will read of God's favor and His redemption, for you are chosen and forgiven. In Jesus, you can find the rest you desire, for at His feet, His joy becomes whole.

Come to Jesus today. He holds His hand out to you.

The Lord with Us

Do you have a relationship with Jesus? The rewards are great, but if we fail to heed the warnings in the Word, the consequences are also great.

Even if we call ourselves Christian, we must live according to God's will. The Lord is with us when we walk with Him. This is the message from the book of Hebrews.

Our Privilege of Joy
A Study of
the Book of Philippians

Philippians is our blueprint from the Father, our plan for joy. It was written by the hand of Paul during his time in a Roman prison, but the voice is the Father's, entreating us to lift our hands in praise to Him, and to find joy even in the difficult parts of our lives.

NAMES OF GOD

Our name tells people who we are.

What about the name Christian? That's what the followers of Jesus call themselves. What information can people glean about us when we put a fish symbol on the bumper of our car, or we wear a cross around our neck? And, importantly, do our actions live up to their expectations?

This book is an in-depth teaching about the ten names of God.

THE VISION OF
NEHEMIAH
GOD'S PLAN FOR RIGHTEOUS LIVING

The Book of Nehemiah reveals a vital truth that our instant society often overlooks. Determination can take us only so far in achieving the goals God has for today's Church.

Winning the lost for Christ takes preparation in both our time and our finances. We become the "right stuff" for achieving God's plan when we are willing to risk everything for Him.

GOD'S REVELATION AND YOUR FUTURE

The book of Revelation is first and foremost a revelation about Jesus, not just the future.

John reveals Christ as the King of Glory, the conqueror, the one in charge of history, the one who alone controls the future, controls the nations, controls all the universe! This is the Jesus who is coming!

The book of Revelation shows us the glorified Christ and the certainty of His ruling over all things. We are not stumbling toward an uncertain future, but we must be in fellowship with the King!

Truth, Love & Redemption

The Holy Spirit For Today

There is no greater empowerment for the Christian of today than to seek out the Holy Spirit. It was considered vital in the early days of Christendom. Now, many times it is pushed aside as "for then" and not "for now."

We are in greater need of the truth, love, and redemption that flows from an encounter with the Holy Spirit than ever before. The Scriptures tell us that our realization of our need for Christ flows from the Spirit. Even before we accept Christ, the Holy Spirit draws us to Him.

The Call of Ephesians

Building the Church of Today

Paul understood that legalism can become a hindrance to our Christian walk and that we must focus on Christ and Christ alone. When our faith hits the road, God is there with us. He challenges us to trust Him to walk at our side through every challenge we might face.

When we do, we become mighty warriors in God's army.

That's Paul's message in a nutshell, and it's vital we take it to heart.

The Twelve

Taking up the Mantle of Christ

Twelve men were chosen to fulfill Christ's legacy on the earth.

Eleven looked to Jesus for the answers to life's questions. One chose the world and the world failed him.

These men were as varied as the members of our modern church, at times at odds with one another, but forged by Jesus into a single unit that overcame everything the devil could throw at them. What lesson can we learn from them?

Our only option is to choose Christ.

END TIMES

Scripture provides us a timeline of events that signal that the end is coming soon.

1. The Church Age
2. The Rapture of the Church
3. The Tribulation
4. The Second Coming of Jesus Christ
5. The Millennium
6. The Great White Throne Judgment
7. New Heavens and New Earth

Follow along through each of these Biblical timeline events.

Anticipating the Return of Christ

Are we waiting or are we watching for His appearance in the skies? The difference is in being ready for His return and risking missing Him altogether.

This book covers six areas of preparation for the Return of Christ.

1. Waiting
2. Mindful
3. Joyful
4. Praying
5. Thanking
6. Faithful.

Are you anticipating Christ's return? I am.

I*Your*nvitation
to*Christ*

Your Invitation to Christ guarantees six things. Once you accept Christ's invitation you can:

1. Rest. It's yours in the midst of whatever comes your way.
2. See. Your eyes are opened to the supernatural.
3. Follow. Christ is your only true leader.
4. Drink. The ambrosia of Jesus becomes yours.
5. Dine. You will find renewal in your fellowship with your Lord.
6. Inherit. The Kingdom will one day be yours. It's called Heaven.

Salvation comes through Christ. God desires our presence, and we draw closer to Him through our Lord and Savior, Jesus.

The Authentic Christian

Revealing Christ through the Fruit of the Spirit

How do we prove who we say we are?

What's the secret to how it's done?

Is it in appearance? Actions that portray honesty?

How do we live out our Christian example, prove that we are who we say we are? What's our authentication, our password, our photo ID?

That's what this book is about, how we can live a real and honest Christian life that reflects the truth of Jesus living through us.

When you finish this book, you will understand what it means to be an authentic Christian.

Unified Church

The world cries out for your leadership as a Christ-driven example of how to find security and safety in Him.

We must band together arm-in-arm, hand-in-hand, our thoughts, compassion, and commitment to each other linked for a common goal we all share: spreading the message of salvation to a world that desperately needs to see the example of Jesus lived out through committed believers.

This book will become a useful tool to focus your witness to those around you and strengthen your relationship to your family, your involvement in your local body of believers and your commitment to Christ.

Mighty Men of Courage
From the Bible

Joseph who was sold into slavery. Daniel faced the lion's den. Abraham saw few of the promises of God during his lifetime. Moses lived for four decades in disgrace, an apparent failure.

Elijah hid in the desert with the ravens for three years, and Paul was arrested for his faith and thrown in prison. Repeatedly.

Yet today we recognize these men as courageous examples of faith in God. The difference is that they took a stand for God, looked beyond their personal circumstances and in faith allowed the hand of God to lead them.

Christ is calling. I want to answer.

Join me today, won't you?

Made in the USA
Columbia, SC
20 August 2024

40354333R00078